MW01630267

30A Style

Florida cottages and family homes along the Gulf

design 360

30A *Style*

Eleanor Lynn Nesmith

photography by **Jean Allsopp**

design 360

To friends and neighbors along 30A

      – ELN

To Peter, Sara and Alison

      – JA

First published in the
United States of America in 2011 by
Design360, llc.
2117 Olde Towne Avenue
Miramar Beach, Florida 32550
www.design-360.com

ISBN: 978-0-9845481-1-8
LCCN: 2010943231

2011 / 5 4 3 2 1

Printed in the U.S.A.
Designed by Keri Atchley

WELCOME TO 30A

The beach is the ultimate retreat. The water is a constant presence, yet the landscape where sand, sea and sky merge is often as varied as life itself.

Florida boasts thousands of miles of tidal shoreline, yet Northwest Florida and its beaches aren't like the rest of the state. And the 20-mile stretch of coast that parallels a modest county road known as Scenic Highway 30A isn't like the rest of the Panhandle. There are no incorporated towns, and for a long time it was barely indicated on the map. Yet a string of beach communities nestled along the Gulf of Mexico between Destin and Panama City flourished in their relative obscurity.

Over the years, the area evolved and grew interesting enough to be a real place – starting with the historic villages of Grayton Beach and Seagrove and coming of age with ambitious New Urbanist towns. Without a recognized municipality, the area is unofficially known today simply as 30A, a name embraced by residents and tourists alike.

Yet even before Seaside drew national attention in the 1980s, generations of Southerners flocked to South Walton's pristine beaches for summer holidays. A hundred years ago, Santa Rosa Beach was a thriving town and Grayton was emerging as a beach resort. But it was Seaside that surely changed the fabric and culture of the place. From Rosemary Beach to WaterColor to Alys Beach, New Urbanist towns inform 30A with an architectural swagger and style all its own with each community complementing the next the way neighborhoods enhance one another in a real city.

The diverse beach towns and individual homes of 30A are a remarkable proving ground of design and a reflection of a better way to live along the coast. This book celebrates the old and new, grand and modest, funky and formal. What unites these structures is an appreciation of aesthetics, a respect for the land and a love of the beach. Whether built sixty years ago as a rustic getaway or months ago as a permanent residence, each is a genuine personal expression, an architectural gem and a place to call home along the Gulf.

GRAYTON BEACH

A resort town that has existed in one form or another for more than a century, Grayton Beach's laid-back romantic appeal has never wavered. The community was named for Major Charles T. Gray, who staked a homestead in the 1880s. Within a decade, Grayton Beach had its first dirt streets and summer cottages. A rambling wood-frame structure from this settlement survives, the Washaway House, built in the 1890s and renamed after the 1926 hurricane swept through its foundation.

A second wave of development came after 1919, when W. H. Butler – the first of a long line of Butlers who have shaped South Walton – acquired land, built cottages and opened the Grand Hotel in 1922. The completion of the 331 Bridge in the '30s made the journey easier and the Butler family opened a general store in 1937. Now home to The Red Bar, "The Store" holds memories for generations who shopped, danced, fell in love or just hung out in a simple structure now with landmark status.

Like all of the Panhandle, Grayton has witnessed its share of changes, yet this town has never wavered from a sand-between-the-toes and cars-on-the-beach philosophy. When development pressures threatened Grayton's way of life in the 1970s, Betty Haynes and other old-line families created "Friends of Grayton Beach." Their efforts blocked several beachfront hotels and condominium projects and helped convince the state to acquire 900 acres of dunes and shoreline that became Grayton Beach State Park in 1985.

Grayton Beach has consistently attracted tourists and residents who savor life along the Gulf, and few communities match its unique civic pride. Whether preserving public lands, renovating historic cottages or building new homes in the spirit of the place, the folks who live, work and play in Grayton contribute to the allure and lasting appeal of South Walton County's original beach town.

In simpler times listening to the dictates of Mother Nature was a necessity, not a stylistic luxury when building on the coast. For many beachgoers the quintessential beach getaway is a wood-framed Cracker cottage with wide wraparound porches and deep overhanging eaves. That was the approach for decades, and it's still a great way to live along the water.

Kelly and Billy Buzzett definitely agree. Although they reside full time in nearby Seagrove, when one of Grayton Beach's oldest cottages went on the market, they wanted to do their part to save a bit of the past.

Billy grew up to the east in Apalachicola with deep family roots in the Panhandle. Kelly is a sixth-generation Walton County native, whose grandparents summered in Grayton and whose mother led the effort to create Grayton Beach State Park.

The Buzzetts' close-to-home getaway (as well as a vacation rental) was built in 1925 by Tuff and Alline Smith from salvaged cypress that washed ashore after a ship transporting the lumber caught fire and sank. Originally only one room, and located across from The Red Bar, the structure was enlarged in time and moved to its present location after Hurricane Opal whipped across the Panhandle in September of 1995. Now painted a complementary shade of green, it couldn't look more comfortably settled in.

Updates sometimes compromise character, but Kelly and Billy added a modern kitchen, bath and bunkroom that blend right in. Throughout, wood details unite the rooms, and furnishings recall summer cottages outfitted over decades with attic treasures and pieces – too shabby for the real house but too comfortable to be discarded. Art and accessories are equally personal. An abstract painting of a seahorse by Tuff Smith, vintage postcards, old books, shells, driftwood, paint-by-number masterpieces, colorful ceramics, and, of course, family photos from the good old days abound.

Interiors resonate with warmth, but the L-shaped, screened porch is hands down everyone's favorite spot. A rustic cypress farm table accommodates eight for meals. Old license plates from Texas to Virginia are mounted on the walls, and an iron bed with a chenille spread invites afternoon naps.

All too often, people have forgotten how to protect and care for old things. An old house tends to a family if the family tends to the house. This story could have ended with another teardown, but Kelly, Billy and their two sons are living the next chapter in the narrative of the Smith Cottage and the town of Grayton.

Cradled by native magnolias, tall pines and saw palmettos, the modest cottage with its metal roof, vertical siding and winding wooden pathway presents a pleasing face to DeFuniak Street.

KENNETH & ALLINE
SMITH
1925
WCB 048

Right: Everything about the house suggests repose, starting with a pair of bright yellow Adirondack chairs on the porch. Opposite: Every vignette throughout the cottage — shells on a table, art and photos on a ledge or the historic marker — is rooted in Grayton Beach traditions.

In contrast to some of the more rustic and weathered cottages of Grayton Beach, Suzanne and Tom Watson's new home has a decidedly contemporary air about it. But in spirit and stance, it surely is a very old soul.

As founder of the design studio INSIDE, Suzanne often teams up with classically influenced architects for clients. For her own home, she wanted a more modern feel without sacrificing the warmth that comes with familiar forms and natural materials. "Old Grayton cottage meets urban loft was my goal," explains Suzanne.

The Watsons turned to architect Lourdes Reynafarje of Kiara Designs, known for contemporary interpretations of seemingly opposing aesthetics. "Rather than focus on a single style, I embrace modern sensibilities and the ambivalence of architecture," says Lourdes.

Working together, Lourdes and Suzanne manipulated romantic notions of the Charleston sideyard house with the efficiency of a foursquare farmhouse. The front door opens into a screened porch that doubles as a congenial foyer. A hipped metal roof with deep overhangs crowns the structure.

Craftsmanship and tried-and-true vernacular conventions define the house. Inside, there's a kind of Southern prose in the simple, straightforward arrangements of the open kitchen, dining and living rooms. Wood-paneled ceilings and walls, vintage light fixtures and antique hardware add layers of texture and character.

Suzanne is equally ardent about unexpected groupings and artful embellishments. Admittedly a serious collector, Suzanne assembles all manner of art and accessories. In the foyer, a painting by Alabama folk artist Jimmy Lee Sudduth hangs below one by musician John Mellencamp, a thank-you to Suzanne after she designed his home in Indiana.

Throughout the home, tactile materials and carpenter details instill an awareness of the past, while the simple geometry responds to contemporary patterns of living.

Suzanne and Tom planned the house before their young son Wyatt was part of the equation. Finishes chosen for aesthetic reasons have practical side effects. The reclaimed oak floors offer a chic minimalist appearance, as well as a playground for Wyatt to spread out toys and puzzles.

It's a commonsense way of building that responds to the coastal climate and culture. But more importantly, the home's easy-going vibe and free-floating spaces are perfect for an active family at the beach.

A modest structure can be full of complexity and pleasing contradictions when the scale, proportions and detailing are precise. A house with too forceful a presence would spoil the quirky quality that is the essence of Grayton. The Watsons' family home feels just right for its time and place.

In the kitchen, concrete and stainless steel countertops combine with vintage mercury lamps,
wood-paneled ceilings and craftsman cabinets for the perfect mix of old and new.

Right: Treasured paintings by Mellencamp and Sudduth create an artful vignette that welcomes visitors who enter through either the front porch or the side door. Opposite: The living room with its antique English bamboo chair paired with Eames stools reflects Suzanne's creative juxtapositions of old and new. The two large prints are vintage botanical diagrams.

Above: The porch functions as the entry foyer and true outdoor living room. The louvered door and operable Bermuda shutter afford privacy from the street as well as ventilation. Right: A trellis covered with confederate jasmine marks the front door. A second-floor sleeping porch is located off the master bedroom.

SEAGROVE

Numerous state parks and protected expanses of pristine shoreline are a large part of the appeal of 30A today. Yet as far back as the late 1940s, C. H. McGee Sr. understood the marketing potential of the area's unique coastal landscape. He coined the phrase, "Seagrove Beach – Where Nature Did Its Best," and set out to develop 160 acres of scrub oak on a forty-five-foot bluff overlooking a pristine stretch of coastline and Gulf.

Many of the local landmarks that define Seagrove today were part of McGee's vision, including the Seagrove Village Market and a host of summer cottages. Margaret and Paul Benedict built the first of two duplexes in 1952 that would grow into the Seagrove Villas Motel on land he sold to them.

Over the next three decades, Seagrove grew with the construction of more homes along the beach and amid the sheltering trees. As coastal development exploded in the mid-1980s, Seagrove witnessed its own growth spurt with multifamily projects. Local opposition to a high-rise condominium completed in 1985 prompted the enactment of a fifty-foot height restriction in South Walton, which has helped protect the character of 30A.

Like Grayton Beach to the west, Seagrove's history as a resort reaches back nearly a century. Seagrove's old hotel and a dance hall from the 1920s no longer stand, yet the community takes pride in its own old-fashioned way of life and still unpaved roads that wind around towering live oaks.

Change has altered the face of the historic resort community, and grander homes now stand alongside simple wooden cottages and concrete-block bungalows. Yet with each passing summer, Seagrove still continues to foster memories for the next wave of tourists and locals who call the beach town home.

Have you ever driven down a street on a regular basis and then one day see a house that you've never noticed before? It looks so comfortably ensconced in the neighborhood that you tell yourself it must have always been there. That's the way it was with Paige and Mark Schnell's Seagrove cottage.

A talented pair of designers (she's an interior designer and he's an urban planner), they went the extra mile to make one such house feel right at home. Literally.

When Paige and Mark heard the historic Point Washington Methodist Church was selling its parsonage to make way for a new fellowship building, it got them thinking about their plans to build a new home from scratch. "We wanted to be environmentally responsible," explains Paige. "And started thinking about sustainable options."

Long before there was a green design movement, relocating structures was just a practical way of recycling both the materials and the labor invested in the construction. "Moving a house is a lot more common than you would think," Paige adds. "If the house had been demolished it would have all ended up in a landfill."

Once they bought the parsonage, they had six months to move it. The structure is forty-two feet wide, requiring a bigger site than a typical lot along 30A. "We found a 120x150-foot wooded lot, walked the property and marked the big trees ourselves," recalls Mark.

Paige and Mark embraced the character and materials of the cottage and added their imprint and commitment to sustainable design. They retained the original configuration of rooms, while opting for maximum light, volume and character. The existing eight-foot-high sheetrock ceiling in the living area was stripped away, exposing structural trusses and rafters. New wide-plank wood paneling added a layer of insulation and character. A crisp coat of white paint combined with uncovered HVAC ducts enhances the loft-like feel of the space.

The entire structure was reused, and even the old kitchen cabinets were refurbished as storage in the laundry room. "When we dismantled them we noticed 'preacher's house' was written on the back of the panels," laughs Paige. The hardwood floors were in great condition so they kept them as they were.

The awning that now shades the front window was crafted from a carport that wasn't worth moving from the original site. Even the old picket fence was recycled for use in the garden pavilion.

Their inspired collaboration reflects energetic style and absolute comfort. Inside and out, their thoughtful renovation proves that looking back offers a great way to move ahead.

*A vintage glider and side chairs painted fire-engine red and a medley
of colorful accent pillows revive the renovated cottage's screened porch.*

The Used World
HAVEN KIMMEL

Above: The drama of the little cottage unfolds to feel larger than its actual dimensions thanks to soaring ceilings and exposed structural members. A new cut-through opens up the kitchen. Opposite: Paige's talents shine in artful cameos throughout the house.

Above: It's all about the composition. Paige laid out a dozen vintage picture frames on the floor to consider for artwork. She liked the look of the empty frames and mounted an arrangement in the living room. Opposite top: A painting by local artist Justin Gaffrey hangs above the bed in the master. Left: The house was reoriented and now faces south, which prompted the addition of an awning to shade the front bedroom window.

SEASIDE

Long before County Road 30A even existed, the emerald waters of the Gulf and the whisper of waves on the soft white sand lured Southerners to this unique stretch of beach. One such visitor was J.S. Smolian, who purchased an eighty-acre tract just west of Seagrove in 1946 with the vision to build a summer camp for the employees of his Birmingham department store. While Mr. Smolian's dream never materialized, thirty-five years later his grandson would transform the land into a holiday town, Seaside, prompting a return to traditional urban planning and inspiring a whole new way of building along the beach.

When Robert and Daryl Davis set out to create an old-fashioned town from scratch in the late 1970s there was no model. After exploring Southern towns in a red Pontiac convertible and honing their ideas, the Davises met husband-and-wife architects Andres Duany and Elizabeth Plater-Zyberk of Miami. Their collaborations generated Seaside's master plan and guidelines and laid the foundation to recapture the Florida of Robert's childhood, a world that was all all too quickly disappearing.

Although Seaside's historical references, picket fences and pedestrian-friendly streets hardly seem avant-garde today, at the time the concept was a radical departure from the accepted formula of high-rise resort development. Instead, Seaside is a negotiation of architecture in response to its coastal landscape. Homes engage the neighborhood, and urban spaces create places for spontaneous gatherings.

Countless articles about Seaside appeared in scholarly design journals and the popular press, and Hollywood deemed the picture-perfect aesthetic fitting for the 1998 movie *The Truman Show*. Yet at thirty and counting, Seaside is clearly more than a movie set or architectural experiment or even a popular vacation destination. It's all grown up with the complexities and contradictions of any real place.

Stylistic currents ebb and flow all along 30A, but the appeal of Seaside never wavers. It's original. It's quirky. It's authentic. And there's no place quite like it.

At Home with Seaside Style

This is a beach house. There's no denying that fact. Yet it's hardly a conventional cottage by the sea.

Robust architectural imagery coupled with a presence that politely stands along the water's edge renders the structure an intriguing gateway to Seaside. Designed more than fifteen years ago by the world-famous Italian architect Aldo Rossi, it is now the home of town founders Robert and Daryl Davis.

The building is only one of a handful completed by Rossi in the United States before his untimely death in 1997. Characteristic of the architect's body of work, the strength of this home lies in an imaginative manipulation of recognizable materials and shapes to create unforgettable images. A formal symmetrical stance and stripped-down classical orders set up expectations and celebrate tradition.

Over the course of Seaside's thirty-year history, Daryl and Robert have lived in four houses, starting with a modest yellow cottage. In its time, each has reflected Robert and Daryl's personal aesthetic and aspirations for a small town coming of age.

For renovations to this extolled structure on the Gulf, the Davises enlisted architect Cheryl Troxel of Florida Haus and Erica Pierce of Pizitz Home & Cottage, who gladly deferred to the home's original intentions. In the spirit of an authentic classic, interiors are serene and harmonious with a monochromatic palette drenched with light from the multiplicity of windows.

"Our home has always communicated a vision of architecture and interior design," says Daryl. "But it's also reflective of living at the beach at different stages of one's life." The home's inherent tranquility supplied a blank canvas to experiment with the quintessential Seaside Style.

The arrangement of rooms splices traditional values with contemporary sensibilities for the most congenial spatial pleasures. "We tend to cook with friends and family, not for them," says Robert. "Everyone can participate and then we retire to the dining room." Accordingly, the living room and kitchen share a central space, while the dining table occupies a separate room with minimal visual interruptions.

From their first home on Tupelo Street to this architectural icon, Daryl and Robert seem to have come full circle just as the town has grown westward and matured. Intrinsically coupled to the original vision for Seaside, their current residence is refreshingly straightforward in appearance but complex in content.

Elegant proportions, exact details and a Spartan decor instill a larger-than-life charm. It's a triumph of substance and the perfect reflection of Seaside Style.

A presence that politely stands along the water's edge, this rigorously planned house displays a robust exterior with memorable architectural imagery without overwhelming the native landscape.

Right: Unadorned columns frame vistas out from the second-floor porch to Natchez Pavilion. Natural wicker chairs and a simple bleached wooden table defer to the majestic setting. Opposite: The dining room resides at the top of the stairway, and the striking white palette announces that this is a beach house and issues a refreshing counterpoint to the setting on view through a trio of French doors.

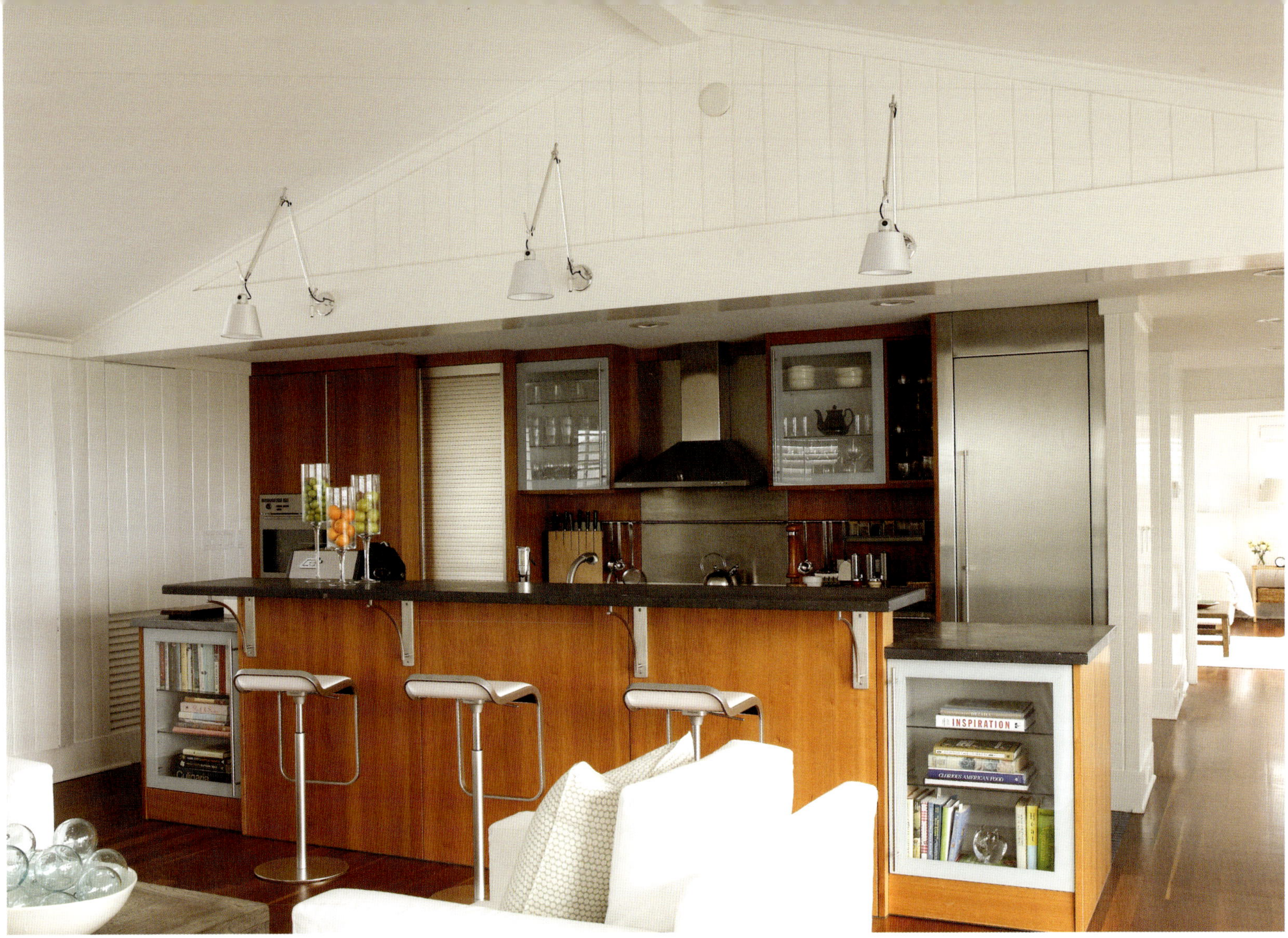
INSPIRATION
GLORIOUS AMERICAN FOOD

INSPIRATION

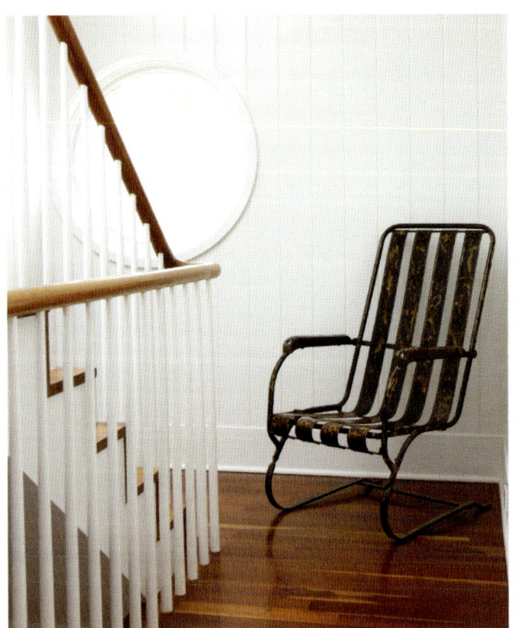

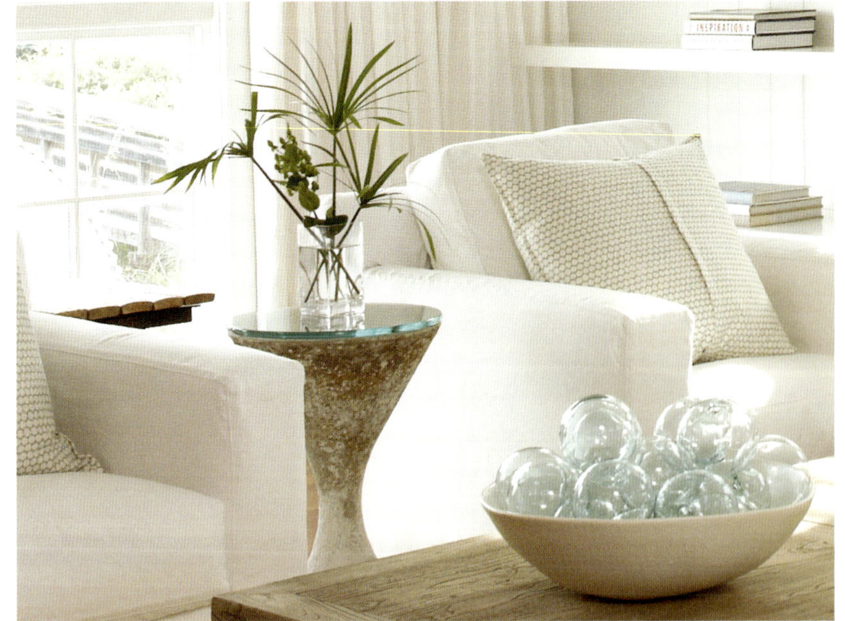

Above: The living room enjoys an equal measure of humility and grandeur, all the while possessing a character all its own. Furniture and accessories are pruned to the bare necessities. Simple bookshelves and repetitive square windows line one wall. Opposite top: The room's vaulted ceiling drops down to delineate the serious and utterly efficient galley kitchen. A mix of dark woods, stainless steel appliances and a bar-height counter creates a sense of separation while encouraging interaction. Far left: On the stairway landing rests a vintage metal chair that belonged to Robert's grandfather, Mr. J. S. Smolian, who originally owned the land that became Seaside.

Left: The master suite features a tranquil and soothing sitting area that soaks in the morning light through floor-to-ceiling windows overlooking the Gulf. Opposite: The appeal of this house lies in its precise arrangement of everyday shapes and symbols to create a memorable image of home. The monumental exterior is a testament to the architect's preference for simple materials and forms. Far right: An overscaled pilaster and a pair of Greek Doric columns mark the front door.

Oftentimes the best part of a beach house is the screened porch. Barbara Bradley Baekgaard would certainly agree. Although hers isn't the typical front-and-center variety, it couldn't be better. Running along the south side of the cottage under sloping eaves, the porch is filled with classic rattan chairs and a day bed that overflows with pillows.

The cottage is a block from the Gulf, yet Barbara looked to her lush side yard of scrub oaks and magnolias for inspiration, feathering her nest in browns and greens with splashes of soft blues and sandy neutrals thrown in for good measure.

"I love mixing patterns and color," says Barbara. And you wouldn't expect anything less from the cofounder of Vera Bradley, the popular line of vivid quilted luggage, handbags and accessories, named for her mother.

Although Barbara grew up in Miami, she had never visited the Panhandle until 2004 when she joined her daughter Amy's family on spring break. "I immediately fell in love with Seaside's old-fashioned feel and the fact that you can walk everywhere," says Barbara. "Not to mention the beautiful beach."

Barbara was perfectly content in the guest bedroom until she saw a real estate agent showing the house across the street. "The cottage was so nestled in that I had never noticed what a little gem it was," recalls Barbara.

Drawn to its play of light and precise proportions, Barbara learned the cottage was designed fifteen years earlier by talented Southern architects Coleman Coker and the late Sam Mockbee, founder of Auburn University's Rural Studio.

Mindful of its architectural integrity, Barbara applied her signature style with light touches and minor changes. First, she painted everything white inside. "But I love cozy and the quickest way to add character is wallpaper," Barbara maintains.

The house comprises only 1,600 square feet, but four sets of French doors embracing the twelve-foot-deep porch make for larger living. "Growing up, my brother was disabled so Mother came up with the idea of a swinging bed so all us children could pile in together and make it fun for him," recalls Barbara. She carries on the tradition, and it's a favorite spot for her own grandchildren.

Amid the patterns, one recurring theme stands out. "I've always loved birds in fabrics and accessories," Barbara admits. "When my oldest grandson Christopher was two, he would point to something and say 'Grandma's birdie.'" The name stuck. Settled in amid sheltering oaks, Birdie's is the perfect perch to watch for a flock of shore birds or grandchildren – close enough and just far enough away.

*At every opportunity, French doors swing open to blur the
lines between inside and out on this gracious side porch.*

Right: Shore bird prints brighten a corner of the living room. Opposite: The stairway railing reflects the home's unique architectural details. Top left: Barbara transformed a lean-to porch off the master bath into a fresh-air spa with an antique tub. Bottom left: A window above the kitchen sink opens onto the porch.

BIRDIE'S
FT. WAYNE, IN

Right: A bright red Bermuda shutter and an exaggerated overhanging roofline define the front of the cottage. Opposite: A seemingly random pattern of angled railings and supports enliven the side porch.

With natural light pouring through expansive French doors and windows, the Ruskin Place home of Sandi Fiske and Jerry Anderson exudes a composed serenity and a warm openness. At once contextual and contemporary, the building feels right at home in Seaside from the ground-floor art gallery to the rooftop terrace.

When Sandi and Jerry decided to move to the beach after years in Washington, D.C., they considered numerous options. They found a corner lot in Ruskin Place to their liking. "We wanted something a bit edgy, but at the same time I knew I wanted to capture the spirit of the island of Santorini, Greece, with its white-washed masonry and bright-blue roofs and shutters," Sandi recalls.

They turned to architects Cheryl Troxel and Ty Nunn of the firm Florida Haus to translate their dreams into a home. Cheryl and Sandi had met casually at a party and immediately connected. After Sandi and Jerry toured several of Cheryl's decidedly more contemporary coastal homes, it was obvious their aesthetic outlooks were also a perfect fit. "Cheryl listened, instinctively understood and shaped the vision," recounts Jerry. "And she always knew best."

The dimensions of the lot dictated the plan, and its location along Ruskin Place prompted the placement of the main living space on the third floor.

"The inverted arrangement offers more privacy and allows for easier access to the roof deck with views of the Gulf," explains Jerry. Including the ground-floor gallery, the house encompasses 3,300 square feet. "We live in 2,300 square feet but all the porches make it feel a lot larger," adds Jerry.

Second homes in Seaside are often designed as though the vacation never ends, but this house was not intended to be a rental. "Everything was planned as a permanent residence for our family," adds Sandi. The location was also perfect since their daughter was enrolled in the Seaside Community Middle School.

Prompted by its vertical arrangement, upward circulation is integral to the function and form of this house. A contemporary stairway of wood and steel rises as the anchor from which an open and airy living room unfolds on the third floor. On the higher level, a private retreat accesses a rooftop terrace, the crowning touch of a contemporary townhouse in the heart of Seaside.

A black-and-white wool rug sets the stage for a pleasing mix of antique furnishings, a glass-top cocktail table, a practical slipcovered sofa and contemporary art in the living room.

Right: A bold abstract painting by the architect establishes the color scheme in the den and prompted the selection of a pair of granny apple green lounge chairs and ottoman. Left: The dining room is an artful interpretation of less is more.

Right: Against an azure-blue sky, the exterior reflects Seaside's traditional design aesthetics and the spirit of Santorini. Deep covered porches engage Ruskin Place. Above: The metal stairway railing offers a contemporary backdrop in the living room. Left: Vignettes throughout combine tradition with contemporary touches. A carved Buddha stands guard in the foyer.

Every detail of this Seaside house was carefully considered before the first architectural sketch was drawn. And Eleanor and Claude Estes happily did their homework in advance. After vacationing along 30A for years, they bought a prime Gulf-front property in Seaside and began their research in earnest. "We rented several large houses right on the beach to get first-hand experience," recalls Eleanor.

Even before the first meeting with Cooper Johnson Smith Architects, Eleanor and Claude had compiled multiple journals with images and ideas. Although the couple had never built a custom home, they had some pretty strong opinions about what they wanted. Placing the living room on the top floor to capture prevailing breezes and augment views up and down the beach was a given.

Once they settled on a final design and hired O. B. Laurent Construction, the couple oversaw the building process. "It was a bit daunting at first," recalls Eleanor. "But we loved being directly involved." To thank all the workers, the Esteses held the first party in their new home for them – a lively shrimp boil.

In the spirit of Seaside's Classical traditions, six Doric columns define the home's beachfront elevation and offer a welcoming sense of enclosure on the two upper-level porches. Inside, architectural elements offer equally majestic gestures. A handcrafted winding stairway ascends to a grand living space with a vaulted ceiling on the third floor.

Furnishing a house that has five bedrooms and three deep porches that function as outdoor living rooms was an equally challenging undertaking. "At first I didn't know where to begin, but I got focused and went floor by floor," says Eleanor.

Inside, a color scheme of cool grays pairs with splashes of soft blues and greens in keeping with the coastal setting. In the living area, upholstered pieces mix textures chosen for comfort and durability. Shells, nautical objects and contemporary pieces are displayed. "I wanted to create a look and feel where everyone can relax," explains Eleanor. "That's why you come to the beach."

The house sleeps fourteen so it quickly became a favorite destination perfect for extended family gatherings and special events. "We love our home, but we also love being a part of the community and all the memories," adds Eleanor. They have priceless recollections of raising their daughter, Cromwell, in the beach village. "She learned to ride her bike without training wheels over one spring break. That's reason enough to have a home in Seaside."

The master suite opens onto a generous porch outfitted with seating and a swinging day bed. The bases of the six Doric columns lend an air of permanence to this second-level porch.

Above: The process of cooking is an interactive social activity, so the kitchen resides front and center. Stainless steel appliances and contemporary barstools combine with sleek granite countertops. Left: The scale and massing of the house and the six Doric columns create a striking profile. The third-floor porch is more than twenty feet deep and takes full advantage of the setting.

Above: The main living spaces on the third floor are open and inviting with windows along every wall. A palette of blues, grays, greens and neutrals is in keeping with the coastal setting. Opposite: Rustic and refined pieces fill every corner. A glass-art chandelier by Joe Thompson complements the craftsmanship of the stairway.

Left: Matching mirrored bedside tables and an upholstered headboard instill the master suite with a touch of glamour. Above: The bunkroom boasts three oversized built-in beds and easy access to the first-floor screened porch. Right: In keeping with the home's consistent attention to detail, the guest bathroom features sleek glass tile and marble counters.

"Ruskin Place is where urban meets the beach," declares Laura Granberry. It's also one neighborhood in Seaside where the locals outnumber the tourists even on a summer day.

Conceived as an artist colony in the original plan, Ruskin Place, with its twenty townhouses framing a park, revives the old-fashioned notion of "living above the store." Laura and her husband Michael were drawn to Ruskin's sense of community and found a townhouse designed by New York architect Alexander Gorlin that suited them perfectly.

The four-story stucco structure is literally a house of shutters and windows. Inside, the stacked arrangement of lofty spaces offers a blank canvas for the pair to make their mark.

On the ground floor, Michael oversees their gallery, "The Art of Simple," which showcases contemporary Southern art and his own photography. Laura commandeers the fourth-floor tower. With views of rooftops, downtown and the Gulf, it's perfect for creativity. "I needed my own space so I can concentrate," says Laura. "Our cell phones come in handy. Sometimes it's ground floor calling fourth floor."

Throughout their living spaces, Laura and Michael introduce bold splashes of colors and warm wooden ceilings. They unapologetically display years of collecting everything from globes to cameras to carnival kitsch. "Michael goes for tradition and antiques," Laura admits. "I'm more eclectic and even a little wacky. The fun and color, that's me."

The windows and shutters that boldly define the exteriors are just as essential to the spirit inside – celebrating the process and patterns of natural light while offering a way to turn off the outside world. Draperies are nonexistent.

A partition sets the sunny kitchen slightly apart without breaking up the flow. "I love the openness of a contemporary floor plan but sometimes you need a bit of separation," Laura adds. Painted a shade of granny apple green, the screen offers a backdrop for an antique china cabinet and a counterpoint to the pantry's rolling red barn door.

Upstairs, Laura and Michael gave the color wheel another spin and decided on a memorable salmon for the walls in the master bedroom. "It's a strong shade but it works because of all the light in the room," says Laura. Floor-to-ceiling windows punctuate the southern wall and a trio of French doors engage a deck – the perfect morning spot to watch the town wake up.

Creative expressions and changes are ongoing as the building undergoes alterations over time. The playful and colorful evolution of this home attests to the strength of Alexander Gorlin's original architecture and Laura and Michael's creative flair.

A study in happy contrasts, the kitchen combines a sleek marble island with butcher block countertops. An antique china cabinet showcases culinary collectibles.

SHOE
Shine

Above: Eleven-foot-tall ceilings, French doors opening onto a balcony and a stairway enliven the living room. Opposite: A niche with a built-in bench features twenty cubicles for whimsical groupings and inventive displays in the dining room.

Above: Rhythms of sunlight and shadows grace the dining area. A dramatic chandelier of orange glass complements the medley of painted chairs and a square table crafted of old wood. Opposite: A freestanding partition offers a bold backdrop for an inspired vignette.

Right: The gallery's reclaimed brick terrace and tall double doors engage Ruskin Place. Opposite: Natural light floods the third-floor master bedroom. Crisp white floors, ceilings and trim play off the deep salmon walls. A pair of mannequins, a distressed mirror and a retro lamp reflect the Granberrys' flair for decorating.

The Seaside home of Lisa and Bob Nesbitt is barely visible from 30A, yet from the beach, the house cuts an immediately recognizable profile. A bold stroke of genius, a single Ionic column is the dramatic centerpiece of the third-floor balcony.

Yet for all its architectural bravado, this home, designed by Robert A. M. Stern Architects, isn't daunting or imposing. It's engaging and inviting thanks to its diminutive scale, exacting proportions and the romantic marriage of vernacular coastal architecture and 1930s Swedish Classicism.

From their first visit to Seaside in the mid-1980s, Lisa and Bob were enthralled. "Seaside was thirty miles in the middle of nowhere, but we liked what we saw of the five or six houses." It only took a few visits before the couple bought a cottage on Tupelo Street and decided to stay for the summer. "Everything was so easy," says Lisa. "We pulled our twin girls around in a wagon. Swimming in the Gulf was the centerpiece of the day."

A decade later they acquired a Gulf-front lot and set out to find an architect to design a home worthy of the setting. Lisa and Bob were familiar with the work of Robert Stern and particularly liked his Shingle Style houses in the Northeast.

Although Seaside's design guidelines can be daunting in lesser hands, design partner Gary L. Brewer came up with a fitting scheme: front porches on each of the three levels and generous living spaces with four bedrooms, in approximately 3,000 square feet.

Upstairs, the house opens up and outward with the kitchen, dining and living areas arranged as a grand sequential space with views of the beach taking center stage. Just as the distinctions between indoors and outdoors merge, lines between the architecture and decor melt away.

Stern's office favors an interdisciplinary approach to design, and every inch of the house is exquisitely detailed from coffered ceilings to hand-planed wooden floors. Handcrafted built-in furniture complements the classical proportions and Swedish country theme.

The third floor is devoted to the master suite, but the terrace is too wonderful a space not to share. While the lower two porches feel like sheltered rooms, this space is deliberately open and out-there with nature. An articulated truss offers shading and justification of the home's pièce de résistance, the single Ionic column.

"Inside and out, our home is a lovely little box," says Lisa. "It probably took a year to fully appreciate all the unique details and special touches. It's everything we could have wanted."

*Canvas draperies, intricate wood detailing, copper lanterns and a pair of swinging
day beds animate the friendly sleeping porch nestled within the native landscape.*

Above: Placing the single column in the center of the cantilevered truss sets up a unique perspective from the third-floor porch. Opposite far right: Facing the Gulf, the home's stacked composition of Doric and Ionic columns offers a highly personal twist on Classicism. Right: A side garden frames the approach to the front door, set within a sheltering portico.

Above: The living room and porch act as one gracious space. Furniture is deliberately lean and fabrics are warm neutrals, deferring to the architecture and views. Opposite: The dining room enjoys a pleasing interaction with the kitchen in keeping with the casual tone of a beach house, while ornate molding and a centered pillar lend a subtle sense of separation. Craftsman details and a palette of soft yellows inform the galley-style kitchen.

Above: A mix of tactile natural materials — reclaimed heart-pine floors, crisp white tiles, sheer draperies and a copper soaking tub — instills the master bedroom with character. Opposite: On the first floor, each of the three bedrooms is crafted with the efficiency of a ship's cabin. A cozy alcove and hidden trundle bed are charming and practical. Doors open into the sleeping porch.

Above: The deep porch on the second level creates a true outdoor living room with a congenial conversation area and a dining table that comfortably accommodates ten. Opposite: Along the home's side elevation, four sets of floor-to-ceiling pocket doors recede to take in views of the setting sun and West Ruskin beach pavilion.

Rosemary Beach

A little more than ten years after the founding of Seaside, architects Andres Duany and Elizabeth Plater-Zyberk returned to the Florida Panhandle to design a second New Urbanist town along the Gulf of Mexico. Named after the wild scrub that grows freely amid the dunes, Rosemary Beach anchors the east end of Scenic Highway 30A.

To give the 107-acre town a distinctive identity, the designers looked to British and Dutch colonial outposts, as well as the historic cities of St. Augustine, Charleston and New Orleans for inspiration. The architecture draws from forms and materials with European vernacular influences adapted to the climate of Northwest Florida, while the culture and customs of Rosemary Beach are firmly rooted in the spirit of a classic Southern beach town.

In keeping with New Urbanist precedent, design guidelines spell out building types, materials, colors, and setbacks to create a standard of architectural integrity and harmony. Homes reflect their coastal surroundings and respect their neighbors without a shortage of individuality. Striking silhouettes and layers of details animate highly personal homes and landmark civic structures that define Rosemary's rich visual fabric. Authentic materials and time-tested building techniques lend an air of permanence, and the town's earthy palette of terra cotta, yellow ochre, sage green, browns and cream enhance the old-world character.

Intent on fostering a more sociable and civic-minded way of life, the plan establishes a clearly structured urban hierarchy of public and private buildings positioned along pedestrian-friendly streets. Acknowledging this unique setting, the plan combines two beach greens with sand pathways, wooden boardwalks, large landscaped parks and secret gardens for an intimate human scale and gratifying relationship between the built and natural environment.

With a lively downtown spanning both sides of 30A, more than 600 homes and a substantial year-round population, Rosemary Beach has evolved over the past fifteen years into a truly urban and urbane enclave.

Courtyard houses are a different breed. They don't wear their hearts on their sleeves. They harbor secrets and turn up in the most alluring places. Historic coastal cities like New Orleans, Charleston and St. Augustine are famous for their seductive courtyards.

In Rosemary Beach, a home conceived by architect Bobby McAlpine for Pam and Nelson Gwinn possesses more than its fair share of surprises. Like its neighbors overlooking the Eastern Green, the house presents a cordial yet reserved face to the outside world and only gradually reveals itself.

Offering an ambiguous first impression, a simple gate opens into a vine-covered passageway that leads to the verdant garden court. The drama of the house unfolds only as a staircase ascends to a gracious social grand hall that happily accommodates the demands and desires of a vacation house, while reconciling imposing scale with memorable intimacy.

With a refined composure, contemporary rooms flow one to another with a sense of inevitability. Subtle details and emotional techniques, rather than solid walls, define the functions of the various spaces.

"People take risks to tell the truth about themselves in a second home," Bobby maintains. "A place at the beach invites freedom from conviction. It begs to be playful, sexy and exotic."

Accordingly, the dining room with a lofty ceiling and an expansive wall of tall French doors sets the stage for this home's grandest theatrics. The ritual of sharing a meal is powerful and Bobby believes the dining area can occupy the most vulnerable space in a house. "When people gather around the table their circle creates its own enclosure," says Bobby.

As a humble gesture of reassurance, the living room is a sanctuary of decidedly lesser proportions but equally elegant details and furnishings, thanks to the talents of Atlanta designer Susan Ferrier of the allied firm McAlpine Booth & Ferrier.

A low ceiling painted dark taupe and animated with exposed rafters forms a sheltering canopy for a conversation area anchored with an opulent white fur rug. Sturdy armchairs by a tailored limestone fireplace, slipcovered sofas and a pair of painted consoles covered with gauzy scrim are a pleasing study of contrasts. The theme continues throughout the interior landscape with subtle shifts in color and tone, distressed natural woods, richly textured fabrics and darks and lights.

From each vantage point that this graceful home by the sea is experienced, broad strokes of genius and attention to detail come together in harmony.

Tall French doors with transoms above accentuate the dining area's soaring ceiling. An ornate Italian chandelier, antique chairs sporting their original leather upholstery and a robust limestone table add to the drama.

Left: A mirrored sideboard anchors a sunny corner of the dining area. Opposite: The main living spaces and the master suite occupy upper floors. As a counterpoint to the majestic dining room, a low ceiling with exposed rafters shelters an elegant and intimate conversation area. Vignettes of coral and seashells acknowledge the coastal setting.

Above: The kitchen serves as the transition between the public living spaces and the master suite. An island crafted of glazed cypress and polished concrete countertops complements the quilted stainless steel backsplash and open shelving. Left: The front door is nestled within a sunny bay that opens onto the courtyard. Opposite top: In the serene master suite, the bed resides in the center of the room with luxurious draperies offering a sense of enclosure. Right: An upholstered bench and an arrangement of twenty pressed botanicals occupy an alcove in the home's unassuming foyer.

Above: The Gwinn House is flanked by two others designed by Bobby McAlpine, who maintains that projects with the most restrictive design codes and constraints are often the most rewarding projects. Within a mere thirty-five-foot envelope, this gracious courtyard home allows for more privacy than a conventional suburban home. Opposite top: Louvered shutters of the second-floor porch unfold to take in the Eastern Green and the Gulf. Left: A fountain and tri-paneled copper mirror animate the lush courtyard.

There's no denying that a house says a lot about its inhabitants, and few structures are more revealing than a designer's own residence. So it follows that the home of architect Tim McNamara and his wife Paige would have stories to share. Step inside their welcoming abode and watch an active family's story unfold.

But don't expect a heavy architectural tome from this professional. This house is as lighthearted and engaging as a summer beach read animated with likeable characters and fully developed plot lines. It's also a book that shouldn't be judged by its cover. The exterior of the structure is rendered primarily in black and white and stands politely alongside its neighbors in keeping with the design aesthetics of Rosemary Beach (Tim is the former Town Architect). Yet inside it's a house exploding with color.

From floor to ceiling, interiors reflect a confident use of paint and pattern. A Mondrian-inspired composition of reds, greens and yellows enlivens the ceiling of the main living space. A bold shade of red delineates the frames of a series of French doors and large windows throughout. Granny apple green permeates the kitchen and accentuates an artistic arrangement of cubbyholes and etched-glass cupboards. Artwork and accessories are equally graphic. "No one could say that we don't like color," laughs Paige.

Furniture placement and color clusters afford the dining and living areas an informal sense of separation. A large L-shaped sectional sofa carves out a generous gathering spot for the whole family to gather for singalongs or a movie.

The color scheme, a collaborative effort between the McNamaras and designer Susan Massey, unfolds just as unforgettably upstairs. With three teenage boys, a teen retreat is a necessity. The playroom certainly lives up to expectation with painted walls creating the illusion of a circus tent. A chocolate brown and turquoise palette imbues the master suite with elegance and style and the same vibrancy as the rest of the house, while affording Tim and Paige their own territory. For a 2,100-square-foot home, there's a lot going on. It never feels overpowering or claustrophobic thanks to 1,500 square feet of porches.

With Tim's firm, NOOZOOdesign, in the Mercado Building, and Paige and the boys immersed in the community, the McNamaras have contributed much to the evolution of Rosemary Beach. Local color is a lot more than paint and pretty pictures. It's the way of life that makes each town along 30A unique.

Bold colors and strong patterns inform every room of the McNamara home starting with the contemporary kid-friendly living area.

Left: An oval table surrounded with bright red leather chairs creates its own close-knit chemistry for family meals. Above: There's nothing timid about this eye-catching kitchen. Color rules the day as stainless steel appliances and sleek black granite countertop take a backseat.

Above: A verandah with a fireplace, weather-resistant draperies, and a niche for a television functions as a true outdoor room for entertaining or family gatherings year round. Right: Anchoring a corner of the house, a three-story open tower offers commanding views of the town of Rosemary Beach.

WaterColor

With Grayton Beach State Park to the west, Seaside to the east, Western Lake in the middle, and the Gulf to the south, WaterColor is positioned to take full advantage of the best 30A has to offer.

The town of WaterColor grew quickly after the St. Joe Company broke ground in 2000 on their version of a traditional neighborhood development on land they had acquired in 1927. With lessons learned from Seagrove and Grayton as well as thriving new towns along 30A, architect Jaquelin Robertson of Cooper, Robertson & Partners embraced the Panhandle's indigenous Cracker-style architecture and established tenants of New Urbanist planning while accommodating built and natural elements that make a coastal resort so appealing.

Encompassing 499 acres and miles of shoreline along the lake, WaterColor devotes nearly half its land to parks, conservation and an extensive system of hiking and biking trails. WaterColor's plan also fosters pedestrian interaction and transitions between Seaside's more urban quality and rural character of adjacent Point Washington State Forest and Grayton Beach State Park. Rather than duplicate the offerings of Seaside's downtown, WaterColor incorporates amenities not offered along 30A – a sixty-room boutique hotel, a community dock and boathouse along Western Lake and a beach club overlooking the Gulf.

There's a kind of Southern prose in the simple, graceful look and feel of the town. Venture off 30A into the residential neighborhoods where more than 650 homes are thoughtfully interwoven within the native coastal landscape. Regardless of size, house after house is crafted of richly textured materials displaying sensible proportions and comfortable scale for a satisfying consistency. Each is oriented toward the street with shaded porches and welcoming detailing for a pleasing visual experience.

While other 30A communities might boast grander architectural statements, WaterColor's lasting appeal comes from its sense of place, its refined approach to the art of building and its gracious concessions to contemporary life along the water.

Some houses just seem to say "sit a spell." Yet few offer that invitation with more style and character than the WaterColor home of Jane and Bill Hardin. "Every place we've lived has had lots of different nesting places," Jane declares. "I'm a sitter and observer."

That said, Jane also admits that "we sometimes err on the side of design over comfort." Fortunately, working with decorator Dale Trice and architect Les McCormick, Jane and Bill were able to strike the perfect balance.

"We just love the authentic details and classic proportions of older homes," Jane adds. The architecture nods to the Charleston Shingle House with a deep loggia distinguished with mahogany shutters. A layering of porches and sunrooms enhances the feel of an older home that evolved over the years. Craftsmanship combined with recycled Chicago bricks, tabby stucco fireplaces and leaded glass windows impart the feel of a home that's not only old, but one that's been devotedly restored by hand.

The Hardins were in the thick of construction when they enlisted Dale as their decorator. They all hit it off immediately. "Together we wrote a narrative for the house and started accumulating things to tell the story," recalls Jane. Using old Havana as a starting point for their fantasy, rooms resonate with British Colonial influences and a balanced play of dark and light.

Indoors and outdoors merge effortlessly with furnishings and finishes that work in either environment. Dale weaves muted shades and rich textures from room to room as the plot lines of their "novel" gradually evolve.

Though Jane loves intimate nooks for gathering, she didn't want to encourage congregating in the kitchen. "I have lots of hobbies but cooking is not one of them," Jane admits. "I like a working kitchen." Nevertheless, the antique farm table makes for a friendly meeting spot.

To accommodate Jane's acknowledged pastimes, a space intended to be a screened porch was transformed into a sunny arts-and-crafts room. "Now my projects don't end up on the dining room table," Jane laughs. One of Jane's leisure pursuits has always been collecting. With Dale's help her treasured "bugs and beetles" are beautifully framed and displayed.

Not every designer takes his job as personally as Dale. When a client hires him, it's a given that Dale will be involved in the decor. But oftentimes he becomes an advisor and consultant as well as a friend. Now when Dale comes to call on the Hardins, the most pressing design decision is figuring out where to sit.

Reminiscent of a Charleston piazza with touches of colonial Havana, this traditional side porch is a fitting introduction to the home's many moods that change from dark and rich to sunny and bright.

Opposite: A dramatic lath-
patterned ceiling crowns the
central living space. Right:
A radiant breakfast room
occupies a sun-drenched corner
adjacent to the side porch.

Left: A pair of pocket doors allows the kitchen to be closed off, but the room is a delightful space with antique brick flooring, a whimsical chandelier and cabinets crafted to look like furniture. Right: Colorful Mexican tile, Oriental lanterns and jaunty sculptures animate Jane's craft room.

Opposite: Warm-toned Turkish travertine, custom millwork and an ornate shell-encrusted mirror reflect the master bath's craftsmanship. Left and above: The master bedroom and private retreat share a double fireplace, peaked ceilings and a pleasing mix of dark woods and white walls. Right: A vivid library on the first floor adjoins the craft and breakfast rooms.

Right: Tall mahogany shutters custom
crafted at a local millwork shop fold
open to engage native landscape and
nearby Western Lake. Opposite: Rustic
accessories, crusty sea shells, all manner
of collections and the signature shutters
instill character inside and out.

A cordial front porch greets visitors to the WaterColor home of Johnelle Hunt. But it's the grand curving stairway that makes a lasting first impression for anyone who steps through the front door. Including Johnelle.

Perfectly content in a cottage a block away, Johnelle wasn't looking to move when a friend suggested she take a peek into a house nearing completion. "Immediately I knew this home was for me," she recalls. "Everyone in my family was in total agreement."

Architect Roger Godwin had originally designed and built the house to be his own residence, and the personal attention to detail is obvious. "His materials were elegant and the finishes were beautiful with all my favorite shades of soft blues and greens," says Johnelle. "I didn't change a thing."

She did enlist decorator Dale Trice to select furniture and accessories in keeping with the sophisticated architecture. By chance, Dale was working with Johnelle's daughter, Jane Hardin, on her own home just up the street (and the previous one in this book).

Unlike some designers who have one signature look, Dale responds to the desires of each individual client. And this mother and daughter certainly had different ideas and inspiration. "Jane thought her Mother's home should be a take on 'Hollywood glamour' at the beach," recalls Dale, who was more than happy to comply with an open-ended design directive.

With the air of a conductor who leads an orchestra through the intricacies of a symphony, Dale instills harmony and scale throughout entertaining spaces and the soothing master suite, as well as a landscaped pool terrace, loft and bunkroom. Art complements the architecture, and furnishings wander across periods and provenance with a contemporary edge.

However, Johnelle was equally committed to comfort and practicality. "Everything needs to be sturdy to handle grandchildren," she adds. "And I told Dale I wanted a recliner and rocking chairs, a swing and hammock on the porch. Those kinds of things make you feel good at the beach."

The Hunts fell under the spell of 30A in the summer of 1989. "We were looking for a place to start a tradition," recalls Johnelle. "We stayed a week in Seaside and knew this was it." They rented for years and then bought a house on Seaside Avenue before making a move to WaterColor. "Coming to 30A has always been like coming home," Johnelle declares. Now the entire family has the perfect spot for the long haul.

As afternoon approaches, sunlight dances throughout the open and engaging main living spaces, highlighting the elegant livable décor, mirrored cocktail table and muted colors.

Left: A patterned stone floor in the foyer and the grand curving stairway establish a befitting sense of arrival. Right: An L-shaped sectional sofa and upholstered ottoman subtly combine with various textures and tones of creams, tans and soft blues in the downstairs den.

Above: The open kitchen is a play of dark woods and light finishes. The marble island and adjoining table accommodate all manner of entertaining. Opposite: A palette of soft blues and greens and patterns of circles and stripes flow between rooms for an easy sense of continuity between the living and dining areas, as well as the guest suite and master bath.

Left: The scale of the upholstered headboard and window treatments is in keeping with the tall ceilings of the master bedroom. Above: A loft-style family room with an oversized game table, the grandchildren's bunk room and open deck occupy the third floor and take advantage of views of Western Lake.

WaterSound Beach

No one could deny the twenty miles of shore that parallels Scenic Highway 30A is one of the most beautiful stretches of beach in the world. However, when it comes to pinpointing the best of the best in this unique corner of the world, there's room for debate.

Topsail, Grayton, Deer Lake and Camp Helen state parks surely have a legitimate claim to the honor, yet step away from land held in conservation and surely the most pristine and expansive tract of rolling dunes, white sand and emerald waters in South Walton is WaterSound Beach.

With 256 acres and nearly a mile of Gulf frontage, WaterSound is a secluded residential enclave with buildings set far behind the expansive field of dunes. Conceived in accord with this magnificent setting by the St. Joe Company, WaterSound's town plan is shaped in large measure to the contours of the land, the arc of the Gulf and the ever-changing flow of Camp Creek Lake.

The look and feel of homes and community buildings combine the spirit and stance of New England's historic Shingle Style with Northwest Florida's indigenous traditions, creating an architectural language with a decidedly Southern accent responsive to this time and place. Exuberant gables, sweeping pitched roofs, widow's walks, whimsical balconies and ornate bay windows allude to the romantic illusions of Martha's Vineyard and Newport, while wraparound porches, shed dormers, sheltering overhangs and breezeways are a direct response to the Gulf climate and culture.

Equally engaging is the town's series of wooden boardwalks, bridges and sand pathways connecting neighborhoods, parks, lakes and wetlands, and ultimately leading through the peaks and valleys of the dunescape to the beach. Offering solitude within a sociable community, WaterSound is an artful interpretation of past and present resort traditions realized in harmony with a unique coastal environment.

The romantic illusions of the Shingle Style with its recognizable forms and gracious proportions give Teresa and Mike Callahan's home in WaterSound Beach an unassailable stance and distinctive character. Surrounded by billowing native grasses and scrub oaks, this weekend home resonates with a sense of permanence and the spirit of a family comfortably settled in – thanks to the deft handling of materials, welcoming scale, and its thoughtful placement on the land.

Although Teresa and Mike live in Birmingham, they travel to the Gulf Coast as often as possible. This all started twenty-five years ago with the purchase of a condominium in Destin. When that stretch of beach became too crowded for their liking, they headed to 30A and discovered WaterSound Beach, where they purchased a townhouse in The Crossings.

As the community began to grow, Teresa noticed workers breaking ground on a prominent corner lot. "It was the Founder's House designed by Dungan Nequette Architects, whose work I knew from Rosemary Beach and Birmingham," recalls Teresa. "I liked it from the start, but once the roof was in place I fell in love."

The couple didn't commission the firm, yet Teresa admits, "It's exactly the home I would have designed." At 3,600 square feet of living space plus ample porches and a 600-square-foot carriage house, the Callahan house happily accommodates their five children and extended family.

"We looked to the Northeast for inspiration and then reinterpreted the vernacular for our Southern climate, culture and agrarian traditions," explains Jeff Dungan. "I grew up on a working farm in St. Clair County, Alabama, and I'm still drawn to barn structures that are approachable and almost churchlike in their form."

The envelope of the house informs just such a scale and spatial pleasures, whereas on the inside, natural materials, nautical details and a relaxed mix of furnishings characterize the open and inviting floor plan. Deep bays of tall casement windows in the living room and breakfast area create the illusion of a sun porch that might have been filled in over the years. A pair of solid brass antique porthole windows discovered by the builder at a flea market introduces another chapter of an implied history.

Two prominent cupolas punctuate the roofline, bringing natural light down into the house during the day and serving as lanterns at night. The beacons also bookend a widow's walk. "This is my special space," says Teresa. "But with its expansive views of the rolling dunes and beautiful water, it's an amazing gift that we all cherish."

*With its sculptured forms and robust scale, this house discreetly holds its own, all
the while deferring to the magnificent coastal landscape of WaterSound Beach.*

Above: The simple pine farm table with painted chairs and a bench reflect the Callahans' relaxed approach to family meals. Left: A butcher block island anchors the kitchen, and a built-in bench engages the fireplace and the adjacent sunny dining area. Opposite: The placement of the carriage house carves out a generous terrace crowned with a pergola and softened with clinging wisteria.

Opposite: Traditional vertical paneling, picture railings and recessed corner windows combine with tones of soft blues and greens to enliven the master bedroom. Above: The vantage from the widow's walk takes in the panorama of WaterSound Beach. Right: Standing tall, the Callahan home strikes a memorable pose. The covered front porch and the second-floor balcony create a gracious interchange with shared community paths that cross over the dunes and lead to the beach.

Long Time Coming
WaterSound Beach

There's no question that Michelle and Arthur Fulmer are beach people from way back. Michelle grew up in Arkansas and spent her childhood summers along the Atlantic Ocean in Wrightsville Beach. When Arthur was a boy, his family headed to Destin.

When the couple first married, their answer was to alternate between the two seashores, as well as coastal getaways farther afield. One time while visiting Figure Eight Island in North Carolina, they spotted a house that grabbed their attention. "Arthur was sure it was designed by Bobby McAlpine," recalls Michelle. "Right then and there Arthur promised one day we'd commission him to design a home for us."

By picking up seashells from every beach and shore they visited, Michelle held on to the dream – though unsure of when or where it would come true. Years later, the Fulmers acquired property in WaterSound Beach, where her collections are displayed in their own house designed by Bobby, the familiar name the revered Southern architect is called. In keeping with WaterSound's Shingle Style architecture, Bobby looks eastward to Nantucket, Newport and Nags Head for precedents, yet his design stays focused on the Panhandle's weather and ways.

The three-story house combines the classic shakes and shingles of the genre with crisp white detailing, double front porches, shed dormers and a dramatic gambrel roof. The appealing floor plan balances intimate rooms with the grand living room's twenty-foot-tall ceiling and expansive windows with the more informal dining room and den.

Equally as sophisticated is the interior décor. Colors and finishes reflect soothing shades of the sand and sea, starting under bare feet with the antique oak pickled to a soft tone that resembles driftwood.

Michelle and Arthur collaborated with Memphis designer Rhea Crenshaw, beginning with a buying trip to France. "We found the sculptural clock's hands that anchor a corner of the living room at a flea market in Paris," says Michelle. "Our address is Watch Tower Lane so it's the perfect centerpiece." A pair of overscaled finials and a giant whalebone dubbed "Jonah," from the same excursion, enliven the dining room.

Inside and out, the design reflects the sentiments and sensibilities of a classic summer cottage. "Yes, there's an antique French armchair in the living room, but slipcover sofas and wicker dining chairs allow you to feel comfortable in a bathing suit," says Rhea.

An effervescent mix of purpose and delight, the Fulmers' beloved beach house exudes an open invitation to unwind and enjoy life along the water, while the relaxed elegance of the architecture shines with undiminished style.

A Dutch door swings open to embrace the second-floor porch, which takes in views of the Gulf and enjoys a pleasing exchange with its neighbors in WaterSound Beach.

Above: Bathed in natural light, a ship-shape open stairway ascends to the main living spaces located on the second floor. Opposite: In the living room, furnishings including both French antiques and contemporary pieces offer gradations of textures and scale in keeping with the sophisticated architecture.

Above: Residing at the top of the stairway, the dining room is equally conducive to family meals and casual beach entertaining. Its central location establishes an immediate visual connection between the adjoining open kitchen and the formal living room, as well as a more intimate family den. Right: A large island crafted to resemble a piece of furniture creates an efficient layout and attractive focus in the kitchen.

Opposite: The third-floor master suite is a soothing study in pastels and whites. The bedroom walls are painted the softest shade of lavender. Above: The master bath features marble tiles and sleek fixtures. Double doors open onto an intimate balcony with expansive views out over the dunes.

Left: With a fresh take on the familiar forms of the Shingle Style, this new home responds to its Florida setting with deep overhanging rooflines, open porches and a variety of windows. Right: Double porches along the south elevation overlook the expansive dunes of WaterSound and a beach boardwalk.

Coastal Dune Lakes

The Gulf of Mexico is obviously the Panhandle's definitive body of water, yet the rare coastal dune lakes along Scenic Highway 30A are equally engaging. From the windswept canopy of pines that hugs the shore of Western Lake to a sandy spit of sand along the outflow of Camp Creek, the dune lakes carve a distinctive Florida landscape. It's impossible not to slow down on a winter evening when the sun sets against one of the lakes, painting a brilliant canvas of purple, pink and orange.

Fifteen named dune lakes inform the environmental aesthetic of South Walton and offer a recreational haven for all manner of paddleboards and kayaks. Although one of these dune lakes is visible every few miles along 30A, the ecology of these bodies of water is incredibly uncommon, found in only three or four locations around the globe. Because of their rarity, there is little existing research, and even scientists seem to disagree as to what constitutes a coastal dune lake.

Their diverse ecosystem depends on an intermittent exchange with an ocean. Some of South Walton's dune lakes are separated from the Gulf by a barrier beach up to 500 feet wide with dunes rising to twenty feet high, while others have a more direct connection with the Gulf. When the water periodically reaches a critical level, the sand barrier "pops open" and the tannin-stained fresh water of the lake rushes into the Gulf. The mix of salt and fresh water varies from lake to lake depending on this natural dynamic, while each fosters a unique habitat for plants, marine creatures and shore birds.

This dramatic landscape also provides a memorable setting for coastal retreats. From a charming wooden cottage along the shores of Lake Powell to an elegant residence overlooking Draper Lake, these homes embrace the unpredictable interchange and distinctive environment of 30A's treasured coastal dune lakes.

No Place Like Home
Coastal Dune Lakes

Every building should acknowledge its context, but a house along the water's edge is compelled to respect its setting more than most. Cradled amid native scrub and dunes overlooking Draper Lake and within earshot of the surf, the home of Lori and Mark Hadley is ever so graceful in its concessions to the sand and the sea.

First and foremost this is a retreat, and the Hadleys escape with their three children to 30A from Birmingham every chance they get. But that wasn't always the case.

Mark was born in California and favored the Pacific and the Rockies over the Gulf of Mexico. At least until he met Lori, who grew up in Fort Walton Beach, where her great-grandparents started Staff's Restaurant in 1913.

"Lori insisted 'her' Florida beaches are the most beautiful in the world, but I was skeptical," recalls Mark. "Then we spent a weekend in Seaside and I was convinced." Years later, the couple had a memorable wedding at Bud & Alley's and were soon looking for a place of their own in the Panhandle.

After countless vacations along 30A, Lori and Mark discovered The Retreat. "I fell in love with the serenity of the dunes and the abundant wildlife of the inland lake," recalls Lori." It was the beach I remember from my childhood."

For a home befitting the site, the couple enlisted Jeff Dungan of Dungan Nequette Architects and Paige Schnell of Tracery. "I had a vision for the house and its essence," recalls Lori. "But we were impressed with how Jeff captured exactly what we wanted, down to the smallest detail."

The property's shape allowed for a "see-through" house with walls of windows and sight lines from front to back. "I love the feel of a transparent house," says Lori. "It's nearly impossible to turn your back on either view."

The center of social living is one grand space on the second floor, where congregating, dining and the kitchen clearly signal a spirit of hospitality. For finishes and furnishings throughout, Lori and Paige worked in tandem. Their palette is a pale canvas of creams, seafoam green and soft browns. Rooms resonate with a mood that is both refined old-world and refreshingly modern.

This house possesses elegance and sophistication, yet its appeal lies in an almost unexplainable emotional force. "It used to take a day at the beach for me to unwind," laughs Mark. "Now as soon as we pass Montgomery I'm in a different mindset." That's surely a testament of the power of this unique place.

*A house in this setting has no back door. One elevation beckons visitors from the street,
yet the true front reaches out to embrace the majesty of Draper Lake and the Gulf.*

Above: In this vacation atmosphere, life revolves around outdoor spaces. The infinity pool is a year-round source of pleasure – heated in winter and just cool enough on a summer day. A great blue heron frequents a shallow corner of the lake. Right: A majestic archway frames the view and shelters a generous first-floor terrace.

Above: Every space is a masterful manipulation of vertical and axial layering. The best of the kitchen stands front and center within the great room. Functional demands are relegated to a galley-style pantry – just out of view but close enough for easy access. The kitchen's symmetrical configuration and marble island serve both the cook and those gathered nearby. Opposite: The dining area is essential to daily living. A built-in bench within the recessed bay window combines with upholstered chairs for easy family meals and coastal entertaining, and offers a congenial corner for congregating. Top: An unadorned stone mantel anchors the living room.

Above: The master suite is a study in elegant tranquility. A plush upholstered sleigh bed harmonizes with rich neutrals accented with splashes of dusty rose and touches of silver accessories. Doors open onto a private balcony. Opposite: The children's bedrooms reflect a more whimsical approach to design. Top: A bold brown-and-white striped bedspread complements the nautical theme of red and blue in the son's bedroom. Right: Good-humored art and vibrant pillows make for a whimsical and fun girl's room.

Karen and Steve Wagner were ready for a change of scenery in 1999. After one of those all-too-short weekends in Seaside, they agreed it was time to make a permanent move to South Walton, where they had married ten years earlier.

While temporarily settled in Seagrove, they purchased half an acre of wooded property in a residential enclave overlooking Little Redfish Lake. There they set out to create a home for the way they wanted to live and work.

Over dinner at a local restaurant, Steve drew a plan with a studio, loggia and main house focused inward facing an open court and pool terrace. "On our travels we love Mediterranean influences," explains Karen. "Our neighborhood is one of the few along 30A that mandates the style."

An early sketch was the starting point for a collaboration among friends and professionals. "The siting of the house was critical," recalls Steve. "Landscape architect Jake Ingram and I walked the property to protect large trees and native plants."

Next, they turned to architect and friend Bill Sabella who used his considerable talent to transform their ideas into reality. Atlanta designer Oliver Carter helped with the interior architecture, and Karen consulted with local decorators on colors and furnishings.

The professionals plied their talents, but ultimately the home is a reflection of the Wagners' sense of style. Everything about this home reveals a personal signature. A translation of classical precedents, their two-story home features graceful proportions and old-world craftsmanship. Traditional stucco, timbers, plaster and paneling instill a rich patina. With Italian, Spanish and Mediterranean influences, yet far from a slavish copy of one particular style, the house captures the spirit of their favorite destinations – places known for low-key sophistication and appreciation of the arts, including the art of living.

"The studio was always intended to be my work area and gallery," explains Steve. Karen's domain is the loggia, where tall archways erase the barriers between inside and out. "Throughout the year, the loggia is where we live." Karen admits, "It's my stare-into-space room."

Gracious living abounds. Both Karen and Steve love to cook, so the kitchen is part and parcel of the more formal living spaces, which are arranged in sequence with framed openings providing subtle separation. From the sophisticated interiors, congenial loggia, and working studio, Karen and Steve have created a home steeped in refined style and a life in balance.

In the loggia, furniture faces westward in summer overlooking the pool and fountain.
In winter, the furniture is rearranged to focus on the limestone fireplace.

Above: A round antique table anchors the dining room, and arched double doors open out to a covered verandah. Left: In keeping with the coastal setting, living-room colors gravitate to an understated palette of blues, grays and ivories. Steve's "Orchid #4" accentuates the room's tall ceilings.

Above: The kitchen features horizontal paneling and cabinets with a mix of dark and light woods. An oak barley twist drop-leaf table and built-in window seat provide a flexible breakfast nook. Right: Featuring a twenty-foot ceiling and north-facing windows, Steve's enclave is both a working studio and a gallery for an ever-changing display of his large works.

Above: Authentic materials and details give life to
this new Mediterranean-inspired home. Left: The
loggia opens onto the courtyard and pool. Opposite:
The roof is clad with antique barrel tiles reclaimed
from a convent in Colombia, South America.

Land is a great luxury in any coastal setting and this contemporary house has elbow room in abundance. With a mannered elegance, the home of Kaarina and Peter Stabell confidently stretches along the wooded shoreline of Camp Creek Lake.

Kaarina is originally from Finland. Peter hails from Norway. The couple met and fell in love while on business in Africa nearly four decades ago. Over the years they traveled the world and raised a family in New Jersey before purchasing a seven-acre lakefront parcel in 1993. "South Walton is as beautiful as anywhere we ever visited," says Peter, who drove down 30A for the first time in the 1970s with Mr. Ed Ball, the longtime head of the St. Joe Company. "The tall pines and expansive coastal landscape reminded me of my homeland."

After holding on to the property for a decade, the couple turned to architect Tom Christ, builder Buster Woodruff and designer Carol Murphy Rauschkolb. "The goal was a structure worthy of the setting that would entice extended family from around the world to visit," explains Carol. Their son Jason and his wife Celina were living in Houston, so the Florida Panhandle was already a favorite destination. And it wasn't long before relatives from afar were vacationing here.

Laid out like a European village, the house comprises distinct wings with varied gable rooflines, reducing its apparent mass and creating the illusion of a childlike drawing of home, albeit rendered in stucco, steel and glass.

An arrival courtyard welcomes visitors, but only when the sturdy wooden front door swings open does the home truly present itself. Transparent and utterly inviting, rooms unfold like a game of hide and reveal, offering a panorama at every turn.

As an expression of poetic and practical Modernist principles, architecture and interiors evolve in tandem. Materials are crisp and pristine, and furnishings in natural linens and cottons are subtle and sophisticated. Floor-to-ceiling windows allow the mood to change from hour to hour and season to season, while simple, elegant draperies and shades instill intimacy. Throughout, the color scheme is like a cooling tonic on a summer day as rooms and porches flow one into the next with style and grace.

Above and beyond the deftly selected objects, art and finishes, what makes this home unique is its reassuring ambience and inspiring connection with nature. Peter maintains, "A lifetime of experiences leads you to where you should be." Their home is testament to that philosophy and the perfect place for a family legacy to thrive.

At the heart of this home is an outdoor family room with a casual dining table and sectional sofa focused on a fireplace, outdoor television, and most of all, views of the lake.

Above: Open interiors revel in a light-filled spaciousness. A watercolor by Celina's mother, the talented artist Mary Quiros, enlivens the formal dining room wall. Right: A breakfast banquette anchors a sunny corner of the open kitchen. Bright orange stackable chairs and pillows add casual splashes of color.

Above: The living-room décor is refined and reasoned, in harmony with the soaring gable ceiling and the home's play of light. Tall doors swing open to engage a porch and pool terrace. Opposite: The home's rambling plan affords privacy with separate master suites on two levels. The first-floor bedroom resonates with a serene color palette of sky blues and dreamy whites.

Left: Tucked under the prominent central gable, this porch takes in long views over the infinity pool. Above: A series of bold geometric forms encompass the gracious rear terrace. Right: From across Camp Creek Lake, the house appears firmly established amid towering pines.

The approach to Kay and Ward Van Skiver's vacation home is a bit deceiving. The turn off 30A is barely marked and a gravel drive gradually twists and turns. But first impressions can be misleading. And even second thoughts are not always completely telling.

A carved wooden door offers a glimpse into an open-ended courtyard and a series of fully realized outdoor rooms amid the lush native landscape. A sitting area boasts a fireplace and a weather-proofed television, while a fully outfitted summer kitchen encourages all manner of al fresco dining. Even ground-floor bedrooms boast private alcoves along a deep verandah.

Visitors might be hard pressed to leave this congenial spot and venture up to the home's main living area on the second floor. But it's definitely worth the walk.

Once at the top of the stairway, views of Little Redfish Lake and the Gulf are sure to make one stop and take notice. At least that was Kay's initial reaction. Her next move was to purchase the property and set out to make it her own with the help of the talented interior designer, Georgia Carlee.

A second home allows for a more casual layout of rooms, yet this lakefront getaway was never intended to be a modest cottage. Interiors marry the best aspects of a contemporary plan where Georgia's thoughtful furniture placement spells out individual functions that cordially stretch out with a welcoming intimacy and a sense of balance.

To capture a warmth and refinement appropriate for a year-round retreat, the color palette takes a decided turn towards browns, warm yellows, creams and just a hint of blue for a calming respite and consistency throughout.

A mix of linens and natural textures blends with an array of rich woods, including heart pine ceilings and dark walnut floors for a layering of rich finishes. A limestone hearth anchors the living area. The dining table with its prominent barrel chandelier hangs front and center as the touchstone of the open space that's really all about the view.

Certain homes possess a reassuring familiarity to lure people in. Visitors to the Van Skiver house are drawn to its unique relationship with the waterfront. Grandchildren are keen for the swimming pool and terrace, guests relish the various outdoor rooms, and Kay and Ward love the reprieve of the third-floor penthouse master suite. From any and every vantage point, the destination is deliciously spellbinding and without a doubt worth the journey.

*The sheltering screened porch on the second floor strikes a balance between
the bold drama of natural landscape and simple strokes of architecture.*

Above: A succinct palette of earth tones and natural materials flows seamlessly throughout the main living area. Left: An intimate breakfast nook rests alongside a tall window. Opposite top: An L-shaped counter delineates the open kitchen with earth-tone finishes and craftsman cabinets. Right: In the master suite, Georgia introduced multiple shades of soft blues and greens and incorporated a horizontal painted wall treatment.

Above: Adirondack rocking chairs line up to savor views from the second-floor porch. Opposite top left: Outdoor draperies offer a sense of enclosure for the guest bedroom's sitting area. Far right: A colorful umbrella crowns the outdoor dining table on the poolside terrace.

Some houses command attention with their grand architectural aspirations, while others draw you in with the sheer grace and utter charm of the owners. That's definitely a large measure of the appeal of Joyce and Rod Wilson's unassuming cottage along Lake Powell.

Every nook and corner exemplifies a mix of context and personality that defies a label. The style is the story of Joyce and Rod's life together. There's barely an inch of blank wall space. Coastal landscapes of old Florida and bucolic farm scenes reside alongside antique maps and the works of favorite folk artists. Walls of windows take advantage of panoramic vistas of ever-changing displays of nature.

A photograph of just that view prompted Rod to consider the house as a weekend getaway, although they were living barely fifteen miles away in WaterColor. "It's so close, yet the landscape feels like a world apart," recalls Joyce. "And we couldn't resist the live oaks growing up through the porch."

Rather than tackle immediate renovations, the Wilsons moved in and filled rooms with furniture and art, much of which had been in storage since their move to the area. Slowly they embarked on their artful transformation. Naturally, it was all about the view. New mahogany French doors with sidelights replaced a string of glass sliders for an even more inviting interchange with the porch, the lake and a new boathouse.

Joyce loves cooking and spends serious time in the kitchen, so an update was in order. An interior wall came down providing views from every corner of the renovated space – a realized medley of cherry and marble counters, sleek professional-grade appliances, a well-stocked pantry and hand-crafted cabinets.

Décor both rustic and refined abounds in wide open spaces where sunlight dances a different tempo depending on the time of day and the season. Rooms resonate with a cozy time-worn aesthetic of a happy life in an obviously lived-in home. The mix runs from classic to unpredictable, yet every painting, artifact, magazine and cookbook is carefully considered and has a story that Joyce is happy to recount in full detail.

Sometimes a second home is as much a state of mind as a spot on the map. Joyce and Rod head down 30A to this casual lake home and cherish their weekends away, especially when it's cool enough to light a fire or whenever the moon is full. "Everyone talks about the sunsets," says Joyce. "But the moonrise over Lake Powell is even more magical."

The house responds to its setting and the path of the sun. In the morning, natural light pours into the dining room and conversation area enlivened by a favorite painting.

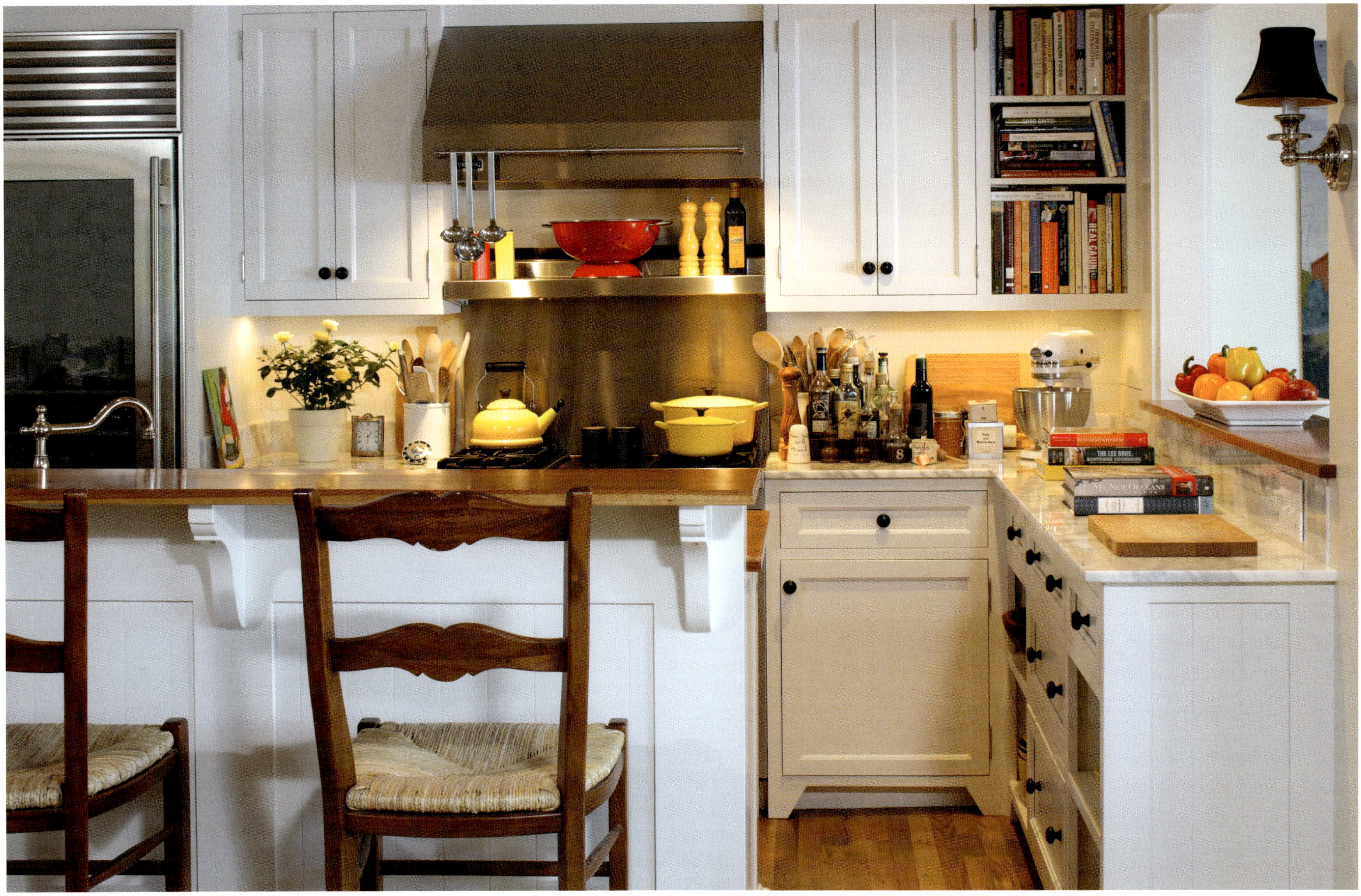
SOUTHERN FOOD
REAL CAJUN
THE LEE BROS.
MY NEW ORLEANS

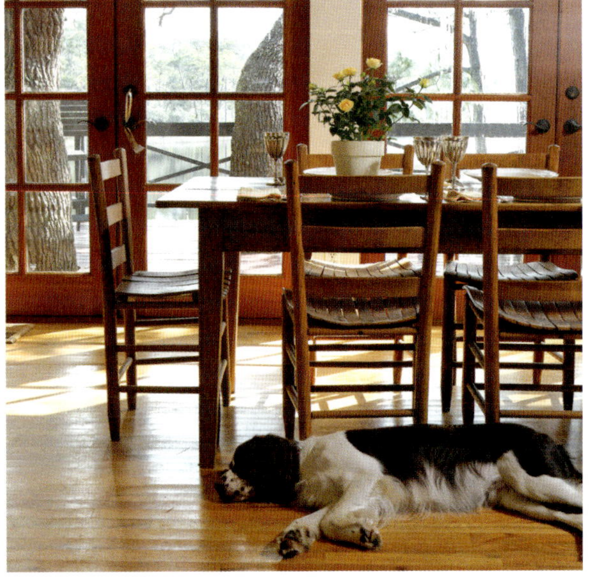

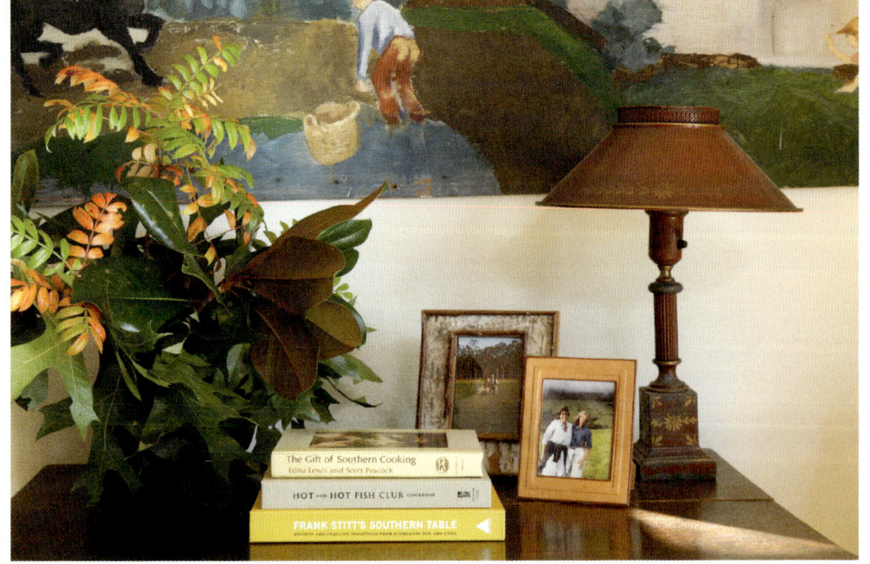

The Gift of Southern Cooking
Edna Lewis and Scott Peacock
HOT AND HOT FISH CLUB COOKBOOK
FRANK STITT'S SOUTHERN TABLE

Above: The many moods and interests of Joyce and Rod are reflected in spaces that are comfortable and inviting in every season. The more you look, the more you see. An antique pond yacht is anchored along the tall gable window. Opposite: Doors swing open to offer the guest suite a pleasing exchange with the porch and its own oak tree.

Left: The new dock and jaunty boathouse encourage all manner of recreation on the lake and offer a spot to savor long views of Lake Powell, the largest of South Walton's rare coastal dune lakes. Opposite: A pair of director's chairs stands ready as the sun goes down and the sky changes from blue to pink to purple.

ALYS BEACH

Offering an enchanting dialogue of classical language and creative idiom, Alys Beach captures the gentle pace of another era and strikes a balance between the private and shared joys of living along the Gulf. Like Seaside and Rosemary Beach, the town's design guidelines and master plan are the handiwork of the renowned Duany Plater-Zyberk & Company.

The town is affectionately named for the beloved matriarch of the Stephens and Comer families. Before setting out in 2004 to develop a 158-acre parcel purchased in the 1970s, the families summered along 30A for generations.

With decidedly mature architectural aspirations, Alys Beach nods to romantic notions of British and Spanish colonial architecture and vernacular traditions of Bermuda and Antigua, Guatemala. This artful vision for Northwest Florida raised the architectural bar from the onset with gleaming butteries standing sentry and Medjool date palms marching along either side of 30A.

Bold masonry forms rendered in white define the growing town, as jaunty rooflines and playful cupolas cut dramatic profiles against a cerulean blue Florida sky. Civic buildings command attention in original ways. Overscaled urns sit atop a pair of classical pediments along the beach green. The iconic Caliza Pool, designed by Khoury & Vogt Architects, offers an elegant arena for swimming and sunning, as well as intimate dining and celebrations.

Yet the appeal of Alys Beach is as much about the spaces between the buildings as the structures themselves. Homes turn inward to landscaped courtyards animated with the sounds of falling water and the play of light and shadows. Intimate paths and grand pedestrian walkways meander through residential enclaves and open up to serendipitous parks and secret gardens.

Weaving sustainability with solid construction, these handsome houses are built to last for generations. Alys Beach transcends geographic boundaries and feels right at home as the latest New Urbanist triumph along 30A.

PERMANENT COURTSHIP

Sunshine bounces off white stucco walls and dances along exuberant rooflines and parapets of the buildings of Alys Beach. Inside the home of Ann and George Hartley, rooms radiate with an equally engaging play of light and shadows that reflect against an elegant tapestry of finishes and furnishings.

Standing tall along a pedestrian walkway, the Hartleys' courtyard house was conceived by Texas architect Michael G. Imber during Alys Beach's original planning charrette and built to exacting standards. "Each home was required to give something back," recalls Michael. "Our gift to the town was a romantic double stairway that engages the pathway like an architectural folly in the landscape."

Ascend this sweeping gesture to discover the architect's contribution to the Hartleys – a soaring loft-style salon in the tradition of a European piano nobile. "From the first sketch, we loved the open floor plan for our casual lifestyle, the mix of materials and the sculptural forms of stairs," recalls Ann. "On a practical level, we appreciated storage for boogie boards, bikes and all the fun stuff that comes with living at the beach."

An ongoing relationship with the great outdoors is essential to the overall mood of every home in Alys Beach. The Hartleys' home, with a shaded rear terrace featuring an outdoor fireplace and sheltered porch overlooking the central courtyard, takes advantage of this natural connection to nature.

Interiors merge refinement with just enough relaxation. Rich interior finishes and gracious volumes lay the foundation for Ann's assemblage of furniture and artifacts from travels around the world. "Mixing a pair of Italian armchairs with a Mexican altar table and a contemporary glass cocktail table just seems to make sense," says Ann.

More than eleven years ago, Ann and George relocated from Dallas and bought the Seagrove Village Market and transformed the local staple into one of 30A's most popular casual cafes. In 2008, when the couple migrated to Alys Beach, they became the town's second full-time family and owners of the first restaurant, George's. "Wherever we live we tend to be involved both personally and professionally," says Ann. "Everything about Alys Beach is a fit for us."

And the feeling is mutual. The architecture grants gestures of friendship, but it's the personalities of Ann and George that give this courtyard home its unique brand of warmth and welcome and so perfectly reflects one family's contributions and connections to Alys Beach and all of 30A.

The second-floor porch offers an ongoing interchange between the main living spaces and the landscaped courtyard, as well as a sunny haven for their Boston Terriers.

Left: An open plan establishes a congenial flow between the dining area and kitchen, while its soaring teak ceiling, Venetian plaster walls and graceful archways exude a certain formality. Above: The living room blends refinement and tropical relaxation and reflects Ann's wandering eye for style and sophistication without sacrificing comfort and grace. Right: Lulu is always ready for her close-up.

Above: Renowned architects from around the world designed sixteen courtyard homes that line Alys Beach's first pedestrian pathway and set the tone for the emerging community. Right: The arched entryway and sheltering doorway open into the home's courtyard, while the symmetrical stairways beckon visitors upstairs with a bit of pomp and circumstance.

Compound Interest
Alys Beach

A beach house isn't like other houses. From the grandest of dwellings to the simplest of cottages an inherent change of attitude abounds in a retreat along the water.

"A resort town should be better than where you come from," maintains Alabama architect Gary Justiss. "It's an escape from the mundane, and clients are willing to be adventurous." That's certainly the case with Maureen and John Fiacco's gracious compound home in Alys Beach.

"We moved to Atlanta fifteen years ago and were landlocked," recalls John. "We set out to find a beach town." The couple checked out the Atlantic coast before discovering 30A. After numerous vacation rentals, it was time for a permanent mooring.

"Alys Beach was in the early stages," says John. "The town's master plan was stunning and it was coming together like nothing we had ever seen before."

One of Gary's early houses caught their attention. "Alys Beach's design aesthetic is based on Bermudan architecture and the planning precedent is inspired by courtyards of Antigua, Guatemala," explains Gary, who designed this home after attending a charrette in Miami and incorporated Deco Moderne elements.

The vibe was right in line with the Fiaccos' vision. "We love the Latin flavor of South Beach in terms of the architecture and party atmosphere," adds Maureen.

Connecting with nature is a large part of the allure of Alys Beach. Four two-story pavilions turn inward onto a courtyard, allowing the architecture to reveal itself slowly through passages between outdoor and indoor spaces that are sentimental and modern, yet utterly practical.

The largest of the four freestanding structures is the social wing outfitted with furnishings and finishes by designer Erika McPherson Powell. Paintings throughout were selected by the Fiaccos' daughter, Christine, an art consultant.

A master wing, guesthouse and "Kids Club" round out the compound. All told, the house sleeps thirty-one when the hide-a-beds unfold. And the Fiaccos love nothing more than pushing the envelope for a party or holiday.

As satisfying as the interiors are, the outdoors beckon. Gary's arrangement carves out grand and intimate fresh-air rooms for every season. Shaded arcades offer respite from the sun. The roof terrace captures breezes all summer and a sleek fire pit counters cool winter evenings.

Animated profiles, engaging materials and welcoming proportions instill a proud confidence, pleasing familiarity and a solidity that suggests there is nothing transient about this vacation retreat. Responsive to life by the sea, this home enjoys a livable and loveable harmony for the present and the promise of a legacy for generations.

Inside and out, the home embraces the spirit of a relaxed coastal lifestyle. The entertainment pavilion features a second-floor terrace. French doors open into the family media room, and a covered arcade connects to the master wing.

Left: In the master suite, sheer curtains mounted in recessed tracks delineate the adjoining bath and dressing area. The platform bed is a custom design with built-in side tables and storage in the bathroom. Right: Marianne Khoury-Vogt and Erik Vogt landscaped and designed this private courtyard off the master suite. It features Cuban tiles and Moroccan influences in keeping with the spirit of Alys Beach.

Above: Interiors merge ease and sophistication in equal measure. The family kitchen's U-shaped bar encourages guests to watch the action, while carving out an efficient work area. Opposite: The contemporary floor plan offers gracious rooms for entertaining and intimate hideaways. A consistent color palette of blues and greens flows between the adjoining living and dining rooms. Right: An architectural fragment that was a gift from the architect is mounted within a courtyard wall as a time capsule filled with photographs and the Fiacco family tree.

The plan encourages an ongoing relationship between indoors and outdoors with a variety of open terraces, sheltered arcades, intimate alcoves and sunny nooks, each boasting a distinctive personality. The central courtyard features a swimming pool and is outfitted as an outdoor theater to show films on the broad white wall. *Right: Evocative and imaginative, the home's sculptural presence holds its own along the shore of Lake Marilyn and happily fulfills the role of architecture as event.*

Resource Guide

Cheryl Troxel and Ty Nunn
Florida Haus
Seaside

Samuel Mockbee and Coker Coleman
Mockbee Coker Architects
Memphis and New Orleans

Don Cooper
Cooper Johnson Smith Architects
Tampa
www.cjsarch.com

Alex Gorlin
Alexander Gorlin Architects
New York City
www.gorlinarchitects.com

Robert Stern and Gary L. Brewer
Robert A. M. Stern Architects
New York City
www.ramsa.com

Bobby McAlpine
McAlpine Tankersley Architecture
Montgomery and Nashville
www.mcalpinetankersley.com

Tim McNamara
TMc Architecture
Rosemary Beach
www.noozoodesign.com

Les McCormick
Atelier @ 359
Santa Rosa Beach
www.atelierarch.com

Roger Godwin
DAG Architects
Destin
www.DAGarchitects.com

Jeff Dungan and Louis Nequette
Dungan Nequette Architects
Birmingham
www.dungan-nequette.com

Bill Sabella
William Sabella Architecture
Seaside

Tom Christ
Christ & Associates
Santa Rosa Beach
www.christandassociates.com

Michael Imber
Michael G. Imber Architects
San Antonio
www.MichaelgImber.com

Gary Justiss
Gary Justiss Architect
Chelsea, Alabama
www.garyjustiss.com

Marianne Khoury-Vogt and Erik Vogt
Khoury & Vogt Architects
Alys Beach

Art Consultants

Christine Fiacco
Canvas Hound
Alys Beach
www.canvashound.com

Kim Pall
30A Style Artistic Collaborative

Town Planners:

Andres Duany
Elizabeth Plater-Zyberk
DPZ & Company
Miami
www.dpz.com

Jaquelin T. Robertson
Cooper, Robertson & Partners
New York City
www.cooperrobertson.com

ACKNOWLEDGMENTS

To create any book, it helps to have supportive friends and family. For a design book filled with interesting and distinctive homes, it helps to have good neighbors. This one would not exist without the imagination, hospitality, patience, good humor and talent of a lot of wonderful people.

The first and loudest thank-you goes to the owners of these twenty-two homes. You graciously opened your doors and welcomed us in with abounding generosity and unfailing cooperation. You shared your stories, making every house in the book read like a real home. We are so grateful.

To the talented designers and architects whose handiwork is featured on these pages, we offer our sincere admiration. We are indebted to the earliest settlers of Grayton and Seagrove, as well as the enlightened town founders and brilliant planners responsible for Seaside and the New Urbanist communities that followed. Without these artists, builders and patrons, there would be no 30A Style.

We express gratitude to all the individuals who make 30A a genuine community. There are so many, but some folks deserve a personal mention for major contributions or little acts of kindness. Thanks to everyone at Sundog Books for believing in the printed page and insisting there is a demand for a book about 30A. For their encouragement and generosity over the years, we thank Peter Allsopp, Greg Atchley, Frank Nesmith, Alice Stapleton, Boyd Baker, Joyce and Rod Wilson, Carol and Dave Rauschkolb, Rebecca Sullivan, Karen Quina Doyle, Paige and Mark Schnell, Barbara Bradley Baekgaard, Dan and Carolyn Maxton, Brandan Babineaux, Lourdes Reynafarje, Suzanne Rester Watson, Robert and Daryl Davis, Amy and Mike Ray, Erica Gibson Pierce, Nancy Hughes Miller, Dale Trice, Kelly Buzzett, Robin Murray, Georgia Carlee, Richard Norris, Leah Stroble and Willie Mason. And if we left you out, there's always the third printing.

We also recognize everyone who assisted in the production of this book, including digital imaging specialist Delisa McDaniel and copyeditor Jerry Gill. Thanks to Sheila Goode for the author's photograph. We are grateful for Jody Detrick, Carol Hall and Boyd Brothers for printing quality books right here in Northwest Florida.

There are so many facets of putting it all together. The process of quilting together an extraordinary number of images into a format that captures the visual and emotional range of 30A requires the highest standards of design, a personal interest in the subject and a love of the beach. Our deepest gratitude goes to the ever-talented and always optimistic graphic artist, Keri Atchley.

Lastly, let's not forget the tourist and second-home owners who infuse our stretch of beach with their carefree spirit and dreams of retreating from the real world for a week or two at a time. They remind us that living along 30A is a grand luxury that should never be taken for granted.